Sakura, sakura
    obloha jara
jak dalece oko jen vidi,
je to mlha či obloha —
    ta vůně pronikavá?

Distributors:

UNITED STATES: *Harper & Row, Publishers, Inc.*
10 East 53rd Street, New York, New York 10022

CANADA: *Fitzhenry & Whiteside Limited*
150 Lesmill Road, Don Mills, Ontario

CENTRAL AND SOUTH AMERICA: *Feffer & Simons Inc.*
31 Union Square, New York, New York 10003

BRITISH COMMONWEALTH *(excluding Canada and the Far East):*
TABS, 51 Weymouth Street, London W1

EUROPE: *Boxerbooks Inc.*
Limmatstrasse 111, 8031 Zurich

THAILAND: *Central Department Store Ltd.*
306 Silom Road, Bangkok

HONG KONG: *Books for Asia Ltd.*
379 Prince Edward Road, Kowloon

THE FAR EAST: *Japan Publications Trading Company*
P.O. Box 5030, Tokyo International, Tokyo

Published by Kodansha International Ltd., 2-12-21 Otowa, Bunkyo-ku, Tokyo 112, Japan and Kodansha International/USA, Ltd., 10 East 53rd Street, New York, New York 10022 and 44 Montgomery Street, San Francisco, California 94104. Copyright in Japan, 1973, by Kodansha International Ltd.
LCC 72-93534
ISBN 0-87011-191-4
JBC 0070-783727-2361

First edition, 1973

Contents

The Blossom Trail

A personal pilgrimage had brought us to Japan in search of *sakurabana* ("cherry blossoms"). As they swept northward through the islands during April in a brief but dramatic season, Jack would photograph their beauty, while I would try to trace the origin of the tree, note its past and present influence on Japanese culture, and find out if the go-ahead citizens of contemporary, industrialized Japan are still moved by the mystique of *sakura*.

Just the evening before, we had flown from Tokyo to Kumamoto, in the heart of the southern island of Kyushu, to start a modern-day version of an old Japanese custom, *hanami*, or "blossom viewing." But the next morning, steel gray clouds lowered on the mountainside and rain splashed against the window; it did not seem fit for flower viewing, so I wormed back into still warm down comforters spread on the *tatami* (straw "mat") floor of the *ryokan* (Japanese-style hotel) and went back to sleep.

Later that morning, I asked Mr. Akinori Fujiyoshi of the Kumamoto Prefecture Office if people still went on hanami as they once did in the old days. Early records tell of the hanami party of Emperor Saga in A.D. 812 given at the imperial court in Kyoto, but previous monarchs had journeyed to the mountains for sakura

7

viewing, including the Empress Jitō (686–97), who made several hanami journeys during her reign.

"I think now," answered Mr. Fujiyoshi, smiling, "many just like the excuse to relax and have a party outdoors with plenty of sake and beer. Kumamoto is called 'honeymoon city,' and since spring is one popular time to marry, many come here to see the castle and its cherry trees."

Later I found another connection between sakura and weddings when I discovered that a special tea is made with salt-preserved cherry petals, which open when steeped, ensuring the couple's future happiness.

A cherry blossom falls from the calyx after only two or three days in bloom, and this beautiful but transient existence is representative of the spirit of samurai warriors and their willingness to die for their cause. An old proverb claims, "The cherry is first among flowers, as the warrior is first among men." So closely associated were samurai and cherry blossoms that it is claimed that during the Kamakura period (1192–1333), a samurai heading into battle would stop his march if the only way led over a path strewn with cherry petals. He considered it desecration to trample on the blossoms.

That may be one of the reasons that castles in Japan rise above circlets of misty pink sakura. Always built on hilltops, the donjon climbs in ever higher tiers with uptilted eaves, giving it a look of pending flight. In former days, it seems, the Japanese never built anything in a straight line when a graceful curve could be used. In general, castle complexes were guarded by watchtowers above each of several gates. Inner walls and moats were meant to confuse invaders by diverting them from their goal, so today's tourist must likewise pursue a devious trail to reach the heart of the grounds and the donjon.

The castle at Kumamoto is surrounded by the usual broad, water-filled moat, and its maze of intimidating stone walls dates from 1607, but the donjon itself was destroyed about one hundred years ago and the present building, an exact replica in ferroconcrete, was completed in 1960. The morning rain faded to afternoon mist as we flowed with the crowds winding through the stone corridors. From wall tops cherry trees leaned, dropping wet petals that clung to our hair, faces and clothes. Thirteen flights of stone stairs brought us to the topmost tower, that of the donjon, where windows overlooked the city and the pink blossoms far below.

Among the collection of samurai paraphernalia displayed on the various floors of the donjon, we found the sakura motif, etched into ancient metal sword guards. And that is how we came to meet a National Human Treasure.

Inquiring about the engraving on the sword guard, we found that it was the centuries-old art of damascene, and that Kumamoto is famous for it. So highly skilled is the town's leading artist that he was designated a National Human Treasure in April, 1965, by the Cultural Properties Protection Committee of the Ministry of Education. We arranged through Mr. Fujiyoshi to meet the octogenarian, Mr. Taihei Yonemitsu, a tenth-generation damascene artist, at his home. As we made our way there, head-high stone walls lined both sides of the path, but neatly pruned evergreen trees overtopped them, and here and there a cherry tree flared in strong relief against unpainted dark wood houses.

In a tiny anteroom, we shed our shoes to walk across the tatami. Along a small hallway several young men, seated crosslegged

9

before a long, low bench, bent almost double over their work. Tiny hammers tapped a hairline design into the iron. Later the grooves would be filled with gold or silver, then the iron etched away with acid, leaving a mat black surface from which the precious-metal design would stand slightly raised. It takes an average of ten years to become accomplished at the process. Although Mr. Yonemitsu no longer works himself, he has eight apprentices.

Mr. Yonemitsu, dressed in baggy dark trousers and a brown cardigan sweater, came forward; we bowed, Japanese style, then shook hands, Western style. He motioned us to be seated on cushions on the floor, and, over magically appearing cups of green tea, we told Mr. Yonemitsu (through our interpreter) that we would like to take pictures of him and some examples of his work.

The artist himself temporarily disappeared, so we admired the beautiful sakura designs Mr. Yonemitsu had executed, designs that have been passed from father to son for generations. Shortly afterward Mr. Yonemitsu reappeared formally dressed in a dark brown kimono. He smilingly apologized for the delay, saying, "My wife is away today, and I couldn't find a clean kimono." Then he folded himself onto the *zabuton* ("cushion") and declared himself ready to be photographed.

The next day, blessed by the sun, Kumamoto held its annual festival. Kyushu was once known as the "Land of Fire" after its active volcanoes, and the parade was delayed because a relay runner bearing the torch, lighted from Mount Aso's crater, was late. Finally he plodded into view, amid wild cheers from the crowd, set ablaze a brazier symbolizing the spirit of fire, and the parade got under-way. At its head rode the governor of the prefecture in a sakura-bedecked oxcart, dressed in a splendid orange brocade costume.

Suddenly pushing through the crowd (an estimated one hundred thousand) came Taeko, our room girl at the inn. She had been searching for us, eager to translate the banners and explain the dances. Sponsors of the parade ranged from florists' shops and used-car dealers to kettle makers, tractor manufacturers, and sake brewers. There were representatives of ancient samurai—some riding small tractors—countless bands, a group of "Fijian cannibals," children's groups in all sizes and costumes, and professional dancers. There was a lion dance, a Buddhist thanksgiving dance, a successful fisherman dance, as well as a duo of dragons coiling and uncoiling sinuously to end the procession.

That Sunday, we wandered through lovely Suizenji Park, constructed over three hundred years ago by the Hosokawa clan, which came to power after the defeat of the builders of Kumamoto Castle, the Kato clan. Throughout the park and adjacent zoo, crowds relaxed in a holiday mood. A strolling minstrel with his plaintive-sounding samisen played requests as picnickers sat with their shoes off, around spread-out mats that were resplendent with delicacies, including sake and cartons of beer. Above the merrymakers, fragile cherry blossoms trembled on the brink of disaster. One petal fell . . . two . . . another . . . more and more—caught by the wind, they whirled, drifting to oblivion.

It was time to move on, and the next day we were to head north following the sakura trail to the main island of Honshu. That evening as we lifted our cups of hot sake that Taeko poured for us, there on the cup—the five-petaled blossom. We were beginning to see it everywhere. Television newscast cameras dwelt lovingly on the most recent blossoming. Newspapers, including some of the English language dailies, gave front-page bulletins on prime sakura-viewing areas. We saw the design used on headscarves, on *furoshiki* (carrying cloths), as inlaid mother-of-pearl decorations on black lacquer *geta* (wooden "pattens"), and on fancy chopsticks. A spray borders the five-hundred- and one-thousand-yen notes; the one-hundred-yen coin is embossed with a bouquet; a camera film, an automobile and a brand of cigarettes are named after it; and near Kyushu's southern tip, a smoking volcano is called Sakurajima.

While speeding northward aboard the limited express to Hiroshima, I realized that Japan is a land of jagged horizons, with mountains challenging the eye on every side. Farmers tame hillsides with hand-hewn terraces, and valleys are jigsawed into tiny plots, some now blazing with yellow rape blooms. In others, the sun sparkled on the water running between furrows of newly sprouted wheat. Such is Kyushu's mild climate that fields never lie fallow. But nowhere did I see cherry trees growing in wild abandon as I had imagined. Sakura takes the touch of man to flourish.

The trip to Hiroshima took precisely six hours and fifty-four minutes. The train tunnels under the narrow sea channel that separates Kyushu from Honshu. Knowing the to-the-minute arrival time ensured our getting off at the right station, even though the announcements were a blur of Japanese. Punctuality is a point of honor in Japan's railway system.

Peace Memorial Park, in the heart of the rebuilt city, lies in a triangle formed by the Hon and Motoyasu rivers, bordered at the base by the broad Peace Boulevard. Like a thorny crown, the tower of the crumbling Industry Promotion Hall rises behind not-quite-pink blossoms of young cherry trees growing along the rivers' banks. Who had planted the sakura? To find the answer I sought out Mr. S. Morihiro, director of the Peace Memorial Museum. He told me that a group of local citizens some years ago had banded together to plant cherry trees as a memorial. A granite tablet on the bank of the Motoyasu River states: "Memorial Planting for Restoration 1958," and the other side lists the contributors: the governor, the mayor, banks, and small shop owners. So far they have planted 260 cherry trees along the two riverbanks outlining the park.

"And each year," Mr. Morihiro said softly, "they become more beautiful."

In the gold and apricot twilight, a man walked slowly before us, hand in hand with his two children. He lifted his face toward the blossoming trees and softly sang an old popular song to his admiring children:

> Sakura, sakura,
> The sky of spring
> As far as the eye can see—
> Is it mist or clouds?
> The fragrance drifts forth.
> Well, well . . .
> Let's go to see.

Ferries to the nearby island of Miyajima run every half hour, or the romantically inclined can take the slower dragon boat. The island's Itsukushima Shrine with its famous red torii standing in the sea is a haunt of picture-hungry tourists and devout pilgrims. We wondered if we might find further signs here of the sakura tradition, for the oft restored shrine is among the oldest in Japan, founded sometime before 811, when it entered recorded history. It was the main shrine of the Heike clan, who in the latter part of the Heian period (794–1185) fought and won a civil war with the Minamoto clan. For twenty-nine years they were the ruling power in Kyoto, the capital, until they were overthrown by the same Minamoto clan in 1185, marking the fall of the capital and the beginning of a new period, the Kamakura (1185–1333), and the prominence of the samurai class.

Approaching the Shinto shrine, we saw a dance by an elaborately dressed priest in progress. Hurriedly, we slipped over our shoes the required coarse straw slippers and scuffed down long open-sided corridors toward the action. A group of tourists had arranged for a special performance of *bugaku*, a dance out of antiquity, once performed only for nobility and now danced ten times a year as a rededication ceremony for the shrine. Five white-clad priests beating drums and piping music from unusual flutelike instruments sat offstage while the dancer performed in his centuries-old costume embroidered with sakura.

A Shinto shrine is considered the earthly resting place of the invisible spirits, or *kami*, the deities of heaven and earth. *Kami* can be rock or thunder, mountain or tree, animal or insect. *Kami* can also be great heroes of the past, or mythological spirits of the supernatural, or ancestors who are honored at home altars. Shinto is indigenously Japanese, but Buddhism, which came to Japan from China by way of Korea in A.D. 552, is also part of Japanese religious life.

"We marry Shinto and die Buddhist," one Japanese told me. Near many shrines will be a Buddhist temple and sometimes, as at

1-3. *Dancers* (*below*) don traditional costumes for the Hinokuni Festival held in Kumamoto City, April 1–3. The planting of the cherry trees on Miyuki slope, the approach to Kumamoto Castle (*previous page and opposite*), commemorated a visit by Emperor Meiji, who reigned from 1868 to 1912. The castle dates back to the early seventeenth century.

4-7. *The Hinokuni Festival* brings together the traditional and the modern to encourage local industry. Kyushu has played a central role in the nation's history and is considered to be the cradle of Japanese civilization.

8. *Dragon dances*, usually associated with a specific Shinto shrine, came from China through the port of Nagasaki, also in Kyushu, during the later part of the Edo period (1603–1868).

9-10. *Taihei Yonemitsu* (*left*) is a damascene artist and a Living National Treasure. His sword guards (*above*) incorporate the cherry blossom design.

11-12. *A samisen player* strolls in Kumamoto's Suizen-ji Park, but the blossoms are to be seen everywhere, as in the private garden below.

13. *Itsukushima Shrine*, on Miyajima island in Hiroshima Bay, is one of the *sankei* ("three famous beauty spots"), which the Japanese have long esteemed.

14. *The shrine* carries on the tradition of *bugaku*, a dance drama that was once performed only for the imperial court. Beneath the stage flow the waters of the bay.

15-16. *The five-storied pagoda* was built
by Toyotomi Hideyoshi in 1571, more
than five centuries after Itsukushima
Shrine was founded. Many of the
thousands of people who come to
view the cherry blossoms come also
for *hatsumōde*, the first shrine or temple
visit of the new year.

17-21. *Cherry blossoms* greet the visitor everywhere as he makes his way from Itsukushima's principle shrine to the subsidiary shrines and buildings, all of which are connected by galleries and corridors.

22-23. *Slips of paper,* called *omikuji* (*left*), are tied to tree branches if the portents for the future written thereon are unfavorable. Obtained from both Buddhist temples and Shinto shrines, they will be kept if favorable. Below, a woman contemplates while she composes a poem.

24. *Evocative symbols* of the transience ▶ of life are cherry blossoms and the skeleton of the Industry Promotion Hall in Hiroshima (*overleaf*).

sakura-smothered Itsukushima, there will be a five-storied pagoda representing the Buddhist *godai*, or the five elements: earth, water, fire, wind and air.

We flew eastward toward Kyoto in a jet from Hiroshima to Osaka, and soon were descending over the blue tiled roofs of Japan's second largest city and the site of Expo '70, the first world's fair ever held in Asia. As the symbol for this important event, Japan, the world's third industrial power, chose not some abstract futuristic design but instead selected the simple five-petaled sakura, stylized in a modern mode. Festival Plaza displayed a different aspect of the nation's heritage in each petal pavilion.

On arriving in Kyoto, which has some fifteen hundred Buddhist temples and over two hundred Shinto shrines, we welcomed the guiding hand provided by our friend, Reitarō Fujita. In the heart of Kyoto is the Heian Shrine, built in 1895 as a commemoration of the 1,100th anniversary of the founding of the city. The shrine represents, on a reduced scale, a replica of the first imperial palace and gardens, which were completed in 794. If sakura designs had been used here, it would provide the earliest evidence we had come across of the importance of the flower in Japanese culture.

I was not disappointed. Of the two trees standing in places of honor before the shrine, one was a cherry. Mr. Fujita explained: "Of course, always at palaces, the sakura is on the left, the orange tree to the right. It is traditional."

On cloths hanging above the doorways were sakura; on the special imperial sake cups were sakura; on the yard woman's

CHERRY BLOSSOMS ✿

mompe (baggy work pants) were sakura. In the nearby museum on almost every preserved samurai costume again were sakura.

In gardens behind the shrine, dozens of weeping cherry trees swayed their graceful wands over still ponds. *Yamazakura*, or mountain cherries, glowed against a background of black-green pines. *Yamazakura*, I learned, had been transplanted from Mount Yoshino, near Nara, by Emperor Kameyama, after he abdicated in 1274 and took up residence in the exquisitely beautiful Arashiyama area of Kyoto.

The annual sakura festival parade at Hirano Shrine was not a publicized affair. We saw no foreigners nor even any Japanese tourists, which is rare for Kyoto in the springtime. The participants readied themselves for the round-the-block procession with much joking and laughing. Pretty girls posed self-consciously in ancient costumes, and a little girl who had been chosen to lead the parade, an *ochigo-san*, looked bewildered by it all. There were fierce looking horned masks (*hannya*, the incarnation of female jealousy), and men, dressed in the twelfth-century layered armor of the samurai, rode horseback. *Sho-no-fue*, an ancient bamboo instrument with seventeen pipes cupped in the hands of a white-kimonoed priest, gave forth mournful sounds accompanied by a big drum booming from a sakura-decorated truck heading the procession. Kids eating candied apples on sticks stopped to watch, and a bent old man in a tobacco-colored kimono and *geta* hung his cane over his arm and shakily snapped a picture with his prewar camera.

In a Kyoto suburb is Daigo-ji temple, founded in 874. Its pagoda, dating from 905 and the oldest extant building in Kyoto, is designated a National Treasure. Walls and sliding doors in the Sambō-in hall are covered with beautiful paintings, many of sakura, by some of Japan's most famous artists. The gardens have the disciplined quality of evergreen, rock and water, and I felt an aura of quiet serenity as I walked along the timeworn board porches in my stockinged feet.

No photography is permitted inside the temple, but there were no restrictions approaching the gate where rows of cherry trees in full glory of bloom stopped busloads of tourists in their tracks. Every Japanese seems to carry a camera, and picture taking is as automatic as bowing.

Nearly four hundred years ago a famous hanami was held at Daigo-ji, given by the regent, Hideyoshi Toyotomi. Women wore especially made kimonos honoring the flowers, and all the daimyos, or feudal barons, attended. Lavish entertainment and poetry readings devoted to sakura were given. That autumn Hideyoshi died, and political power passed, after some internecine struggles, to one of his generals, who founded the Tokugawa shogunate. In the upheaval of the century that followed, hanami became the springtime custom of all the people, instead of an elite activity of the privileged few. Today the Japanese still go on hanami, but now their cameras as well as their brushes capture the poetry.

It was long before the time of Hideyoshi that reflections of the sakura's significance first appeared in art, and it remains today in the theater of nō, kabuki and *jōruri*; in painting and sculpture; in the literature of *waka* and *haiku* poetry; and in woodblock printing.

Theater developed slowly after the late Kamakura period (1249–1382), first under the patronage of the shogun, later becoming popular among the townspeople. Dating from the fourteenth century, nō is drama and dance in slow motion with the main actors wearing masks, while kabuki, dating from the early seventeenth

CHERRY BLOSSOMS ✤

century, has a livelier style. It borrowed heavily from nō, and many plays incorporate sakura symbolically. In the kabuki play I saw (*Kinkakuji*) the heroine, imprisoned by being tied to a cherry tree, scuffs fallen cherry petals together with her feet, shaping them into a rat, which magically springs to life and nibbles her free of her fetters.

But it remained for literature to develop the symbolism of sakura to the full. Murasaki Shikibu, the eleventh-century authoress of the *Genji Monogatari* (*The Tale of Genji*), one of the world's great classics, describes one beautiful woman in her story: "She is as beautiful as a cherry tree breaking into a profusion of blossoms seen through the soft haze at the dawn of a spring day." In contrast with this elaborate style are *tanka* (of 31 syllables) and *haiku* (of 17 syllables), Japanese poetic forms renowned for their brevity and evocative meanings. Consider for example:

> Before they bloomed, I longed for them;
> After they bloomed, I knew that they must fade.
> The mountain cherry flowers:
> Sorrow alone for my poor heart.

This was written by a tenth-century mother, Lady Nakatsukasa, mourning the springtime death of her baby.

A famous twelfth-century poetess, Princess Shikushi, penned a coy invitation to her lover:

> The double cherry near the caves
> Nearly overblown I find.
> Will someone call on me
> Before the flowers are visited by the wind?

Prince Koreakira, her lover, responded in kind:

> Oh sad! Until the double cherry bloom
> Began to fade,
> Of coming to your house, o heartless one,
> No word you said.

Priest Saigyō (1118–90), a poet and archer, wrote many lines on sakura, most of them more joyous and less prophetic than:

> I wish that I might die
> 'Neath flowers of a cherry tree
> About the anniversary
> Of merciful Buddha's demise.

He missed his wish by one day, legend recounts.

But as I searched into the past, I found Taira no Tadanori's (1143–83) poem enlightening:

> The ancient capital on Shiga's shore . . .
> Alas! it lies desolate;
> But the wild cherry, as of yore,
> Still blooms.

Here was word of an earlier capital than Nara (Emperor Tenji's reign lasted three years, 668–71), where cherry blossoms were already a noteworthy feature of the countryside, near what is now called Lake Biwa. Tadanori, a warrior of the losing Taira clan in the running war with the Minamoto clan, was a poet of great popularity. Realizing that his clan was doomed to lose power, he wished for the honor of having one of his poems immortalized in the *Senzai-shū* [Anthology of poems for all ages], which his poet master Fujiwara Shunzei, was compiling. Engaged in a furious battle with a Minamoto clansman, he was beheaded in the swordplay. His enemy discovered on his body the following poem:

> By darkness overtaken and spent,
> To me a cherry tree its shelter lent;
> As hosts and friends its blossoms fair
> Tonight will solace all my care.

His conqueror presented the poem to the poet master, and Tadanori has his desired immortality in the lessons of every Japanese schoolchild today.

Estimates of the different kinds of cherry trees run from thirty to over four hundred. Just inside the Daigo-ji temple gate stands a magnificent weeping cherry or *shidare-zakura* (*Prunus pendula*). Long streamers of slender branches cascade in a froth of blossoms to be caught up on the framework of a bamboo trellis. The weeping cherry is an early blooming, small-flowered sakura, whose main claim to fame is size and age—it can reach a thousand years. One famous weeping cherry is thirty-one feet around its trunk.

I asked Mr. Fujita if sakura bore edible fruit.

"No," he replied. "Sakura is admired for beauty alone, like a beautiful woman without children."

As we got into a taxi, I noticed tiny golden sakura emblems on each lapel of our driver's uniform.

"Do they have a significance?" I asked.

After a long discussion with the driver, Mr. Fujita told us that the cherry-blossom emblem is the merit symbol of this particular cab company. Our driver had never had an accident in his ten years of service and therefore had been awarded two golden sakura for excellence, along with a seven dollar a month pay increase. Some drivers, however, never get above the one silver sakura stage. I asked if the company had a four-sakura man. The driver replied that they did, but he was the director and he had never seen him.

Woodblock printing, introduced from China, has existed in Japan since the Nara period. One of the country's foremost artists today is Tomikichirō Tokuriki, a twelfth-generation painter, who has specialized in *hanga*, or woodblock prints, for forty years. We had been told that cherry is one wood used for making the wood blocks, as well as being a favorite subject, so I put the question to Mr. Tokuriki at his workshop-home.

"Yes," he said. "Sakura wood is very hard and difficult to carve but makes fine woodblock prints."

A woodblock print is sometimes copied from a painting, in Mr. Tokuriki's case, his own original. Each color area is carved in mirror image onto a separate wood block the size of the finished picture. Each image is brushed with a single color, and one piece of paper is carefully placed on each block in succession. Multicolored prints may require ten or more blocks. "One," Mr. Tokuriki recalls, "took two hundred pieces."

After he had demonstrated his work, he asked if we would like to see his museum. Giving us slippers, he led us through the fifty-year-old garden to a small house. Inside, the walls were covered with antique woodblock prints, most of them of Buddha. Saving the best for last, he took off the top of a miniature stupa, pulled out a cylinder of age-browned paper and gently unrolled a long narrow strip of fine calligraphy. "Sutra," he said proudly. "One thousand years old."

Many of the arts of living developed in Kyoto's artistic climate, and its famous geisha enjoyed a renewed popularity in the late 1800s. We were lucky to be able to watch Kyoto's Gion quarter *maiko* (apprentice geisha) and geisha perform their *Miyako Odori*, or so-called Cherry Dance. Facial expression is taboo, and the all-girl orchestra, seated in wings on either side of the stage, might have been mechanical dolls. The dancers on stage, faces masklike white with prim, ruby-colored lips, quivered not a facial muscle, until one of the cast hurrying on stage stumbled briefly on the corner of a mat. Quickly her hand flew to cover her embarrassed smile, and two nearby dancers barely managed to control their giggles—so they *were* human!

A bonsai cherry tree in full bloom! In the window of a tiny camera shop it stood, hardly taller than its camera companions. The elderly shop owner, groping his way from the murky depths of the darkroom, used all his English to say, "No English."

Before we had left Kumamoto, I had asked Taeko to write several questions in Japanese in my notebook. Now I pointed to the question, "Is this sakura?" and pointed to the plant.

Pushing up his glasses, he brought the book within two inches of his eyes—a nearsighted photographer. Over the top of the notebook he said softly, "Hai ["yes"]."

My next question was, "Is it all right to take a photograph of it?" Again he replied, "Hai."

"How old is it?" my helpful notebook asked.

Slowly he consulted his fingers, held up one spread hand and then added one more finger. After we had finished taking pictures of the tiny tree, I showed him a final sentence, "Thank you for your cooperation." We bowed several times, accepted several camera brochures in Japanese we could not read and departed.

Kamon ("Family crests")

CHERRY BLOSSOMS ✽

Our next visit was to the 180-year-old Miyawaki Baisen-An Fan Company. The folding fan, or *ōgi*, is important in the etiquette of both ancient and modern Japan. In summer it is customary for a host to offer a fan to his guest as a sign of goodwill, as well as a cooling implement. The geisha, nō and kabuki performers all use fans almost as a language. An opened fan slowly brought up from behind a kimono sleeve is the moon rising; a fan fluttering downward from above the head is cherry petals falling. In samurai days, warriors challenged each other with steel-ribbed fans. We watched artist Ikkei Nakano painting a cherry blossom branch on a fan intended for a kabuki actor. Mr. Nakano, who has been with the company for forty-five years, joined them as a lad of eighteen because he liked to paint. For ten years he worked under a master who gave him the name Ikkei, meaning "one way," as a compliment to Mr. Nakano's insistence on perfection. In a tiny loft above the shipping room, Mr. Nakano lives and works before his one big window. Sometimes he paints one fan a day, working until after midnight, or one fan might take a week to complete.

"The design is most complicated," he said, "the painting is simple. But some days," he chuckled, "I don't work at all!"

Kyoto is closely wrapped by mountains on three sides. Driving into the hills, we suddenly came upon a misty mass of sakura nestled in the curve of the Yamazaki Valley. Here the trees, long limbed and slender trunked, lifted canopies of blossom right above our heads. Climbing to the top of a steep flight of stone steps, we came to a typical small Shinto-Buddhist worship area. A young girl, tugging at a bell rope (to awaken the sleeping Buddha), tossed a coin into the offering box before folding her hands in a moment of prayer. As the coin tinkled into the wooden *saisenbako*, I looked more closely, and there on the box was carved the cherry flower.

Nara, the first permanent capital of Japan (710–84), lies twenty-five miles south of Kyoto. Now a sleepy little town with some of the world's oldest wooden buildings, it is a mecca for Japanese pilgrims. Both Nara and Kyoto were spared from World War II air raids through the efforts of Langdon Warner of Harvard University and other United States scholars, who realized the cultural value of these two ancient cities. A memorial service in Warner's honor is held annually in Nara.

Kasuga Shrine with its three thousand stone lanterns and its hundreds of tame deer is one of Japan's most celebrated Shinto centers. Here we found cherry blossoms rendered in bronze lanterns, and in the nearby museum, twelfth-century samurai equipment, flute cases, chesslike games, sword cases and armor bore the five-petaled sakura.

Rain and mud did not deter the hanami tour groups of Japanese. Rallied behind their navy-blue-garbed guides, who led the way by holding aloft colored flags, they sloshed on their appointed rounds. Row on row they marched, from quiet senior citizens, women in conservative winter kimonos, men in wide-lapeled, floppy-legged suits, to junior high school students, all in navy-blue uniforms, all voluble, all eager to try their English, and all wanting to take pictures of us or pose with us.

Between rain showers, we sought out the trees of double blossoms, which are Nara's city emblem. These *yaezakura* gave me the key to the meaning of poetess Ise no Ōsuke when she wrote:

> The eightfold cherry flowers
> Of Nara's ancient capital

CHERRY BLOSSOMS ✱

> Glow brightly here today
> In the ninefold imperial palace.

She composed the poem at the request of Emperor Ichijō (986–1011), who had just been presented with a branch of the blooms at Kyoto. The eightfold (ancient) flowers created a memory bridge between the old capital and the present (ninefold and new) capital at Kyoto. After viewing the trees, we fed the deer and watched them respond to the "Ho-ho-hohoho" evening feeding call of the deer keeper.

Seven miles from Nara is Hōryū-ji temple, a complex of buildings, originally a religious center and still headquarters of the Shōtoku sect of Buddhism. Here, in this, the oldest wooden building in the world, in the *Kondō*, the main hall, I noticed a sakura-patterned bronze lantern in front of a statue of a boddhisattva. Over 1,350 years ago, 103 years before Nara became the first capital, this temple was built by Prince Shōtoku. Although he was never emperor, Prince Shōtoku became regent to his aunt, the Empress Suiko, and during his thirty years as regent he not only propagated Budhism but also initiated the first code of living or constitution; promoted Sino-Japanese relations; introduced Chinese and Korean art, literature and culture; adopted a new calendar; built roads; established industry; and sponsored forty-six temples, as well as monasteries and nunneries for nearly fourteen hundred ecclesiastics.

Meditating on Shōtoku's vast energies, I wandered through the new Langdon Warner Memorial Museum and peered into its unlighted cases at wooden statues, paintings and scrolls, trying (that time in vain) to find another sakura clue. Hundreds of schoolchildren buffeted me about, and one boy extended his autograph book for my signature. As I signed, a nearby group of giggling girls came running with notebooks and pens at the ready, jostling me against a glass display case, waving bits of paper. They squeezed me against the glass until I could scarcely breathe. Finally, I waved a hand in dismissal, and quickly the pressure released as the girls melted into the next room, still giggling, chattering and clutching their bits of paper.

Then we were on board the bullet train to Tokyo, the world's fastest at 130 miles per hour. Sixteen blue and white cars raced along elevated rails, plunging into mountain tunnels, past gray tile-roofed villages with colored paper carp straining against the wind from tall poles, streaking past Mount Fuji, and on into Tokyo.

The Japan Times advised that the Shinjuku Imperial Garden cherry trees were in full bloom with the promised mid-April double flowers. We showed the taxi driver Japanese directions, which he studied from all angles before grinning and exclaiming, "Hai, hai, sakura?"

I answered, "Hai," and off we rocketed into frenetic traffic.

The driver, studying us in the rearview mirror, asked, "Are you from America?" as he deftly dodged a head-on collision with a cement truck.

"Yes, hai, American," I responded weakly, wishing I knew the Japanese for "watch out."

"Ah sō, America, Washington, sakura!" He turned around happily while honking vigorously at an oncoming bus.

It seems the whole country keeps track of the gift in 1912 from

CHERRY BLOSSOMS ✿

Tokyo of a thousand *somei-yoshino* and a thousand *satozakura* cherry trees to our nation's capital. The local newspapers consider the climatic conditions, the health and probable dates when the trees will be in prime bloom as front-page news.

As I sat on a sunny park bench, recuperating from the taxi ride, a group of wide-eyed elementary schoolchildren out for a lark in cherry-blossom park gathered around me in a tight, silent semicircle.

"Good morning," I offered. There was silence. "Ohayō," I said.

"Ohayō gozaimasu," came the chorused response.

"Good morning, ohayō," I repeated. There was more silence until one little boy got it.

"Ohayō, good morning." He chattered an explanation to his classmates, and they all burst out laughing. They sang it over and over again, and two of them laughed so hard they fell to the ground. Their teacher blew a whistle and they started to run away, but one girl dashed back to shake my hand and say, "Sayonara, goodbye," and so they all came back.

Ruffled, double, pink and plentiful describes the Shinjuku Garden sakura. These satozakura may have thirty petals crammed into a single flower. Although trees come in white, pink and a surprising yellow, pink is predominant. When the satozakura sheds, it is a deluge of pastel petals. This welcome retreat from fast-paced Tokyo was crowded with people strolling in pairs, or grouped around mats for picnics, or shuffling themselves together for photographs.

On Sunday at Omiya Park, action under the trees was the theme. Young men practiced judo; tennis on a petal-sprinkled court; boat rowing on the pond; kids climbed the trees to break off the sakura branches although that is illegal; artists painting; and motorcyclists slept through the gentle rain of petals.

Long ago Ninigi no Mikoto, grandson of the Sun Goddess, Amaterasu-ō-mikami, was sent to Kyushu to govern the Land of Reeds (Japan). As he walked on the beach one day he met a princess, Kono-hana-sakuya Hime, which means tree-flower-blooming-princess, so named because she had been dropped from the heavens into a cherry tree. He proposed, she accepted, and they hurried to tell her father. He joyfully showered the prince with many gifts including one of his elder daughters. The young prince disdained the gift and continued his courtship of the other daughter. The father, angered by the prince's rejection of his eldest, predicted that Kono-hana-sakuya Hime's children would be puny and die young: "Just as the blossoms of the tree flourish, the child of the heavenly deities shall continue only for the interval of the blossoming of the trees."

When the princess was expecting her first child, the prince suspected her of infidelity, and desperate to prove her innocence she determined to labor in fire. She gave birth to the child in a flaming straw hut, and emerged safely with her son, who became the grandfather of Emperor Jimmu, the first emperor of Japan. Reconciled by this gesture, the couple had two more children, but both supposedly fulfilled the prophesy of early death. The princess became the deity of Mount Fuji, and, supposedly, the *sakuya* of her name gradually became *sakura*.

While the first emperor's ancestry is wrapped in the mists of myth, his exploits are recorded in the *Kojiki*, (*Records of Ancient Matters*), Japan's oldest history, completed in A.D. 712. Prince Kamu-yamato-Iwarebiko no Mikoto, as he was called in his pre-emperor days, was born in Kyushu. He and his brother became concerned about another clan's war taking place in central Japan, and they sailed with their army along the Inland Sea, suffered defeat, went on to victory, and eventually built a palace at Kashihara. The prince had himself enthroned as the first emperor in 660 B.C., starting an unbroken line of emperors that exists today.

The 660 B.C. date is challenged by modern chronologers, and it is more likely that Emperor Jimmu was a contemporary of Julius Caesar. However, his first palace was certainly at Kashihara near Mount Yoshino. This is now a national park, and some scholars say that this was where the original wild cherry trees grew.

Now we too must make a hanami journey to Mount Yoshino, the original home of the *yamazakura*, "mountain cherry," for we were in pursuit of the mystique of sakura, and Norinaga Motoori's famous poem advises:

> The spirit of Yamato's isles
> If, chance, strangers might inquire,
> Go, show the morning sun that shines,
> Upon the mountain cherry fair.

The girl behind the travel desk informed us, "Every thirty minutes there is a limited express to Yoshino from Osaka."

"Good, we'd like to go there," I replied. "By the way, are there some cherry trees still in bloom?"

"No, they are finished. Come back next year."

"We want to go anyway."

"There are no hotels."

"Are there *ryokan*?"

"Yes, twelve."

"Can you book us into one?"

"You'll have to eat Japanese food, perhaps raw fish."

"That's all right."

"Nobody speaks English there."

"Is there a room available for two nights?"

"I'll call."

She disappeared for half an hour, then returned with a pay-in-advance room chit, which told us that, appropriately, we would be staying at the Sakura Gardens Ryokan.

Once the cherry trees of Mount Yoshino were sacred, and anybody destroying one had a finger removed. Supposedly a seventh-century Buddhist monk propagated the original wild trees by planting them over the entire mountain. For hundreds of years Yoshino has been a favorite place for sakura viewing. Nowadays, children in the area continue the planting program by setting out saplings each year to celebrate their graduation from school. The total number of trees is estimated at over one hundred thousand, and, annually, as many thousands of people journey by bus, train and car to see them. Most make it a day's journey from Osaka, which lies to the northwest, or Nara which lies directly to the north.

Arriving after nightfall to the surprise of the station attendants (we were the train's last passengers), we deduced by sign language and a dictionary that, first, there were no taxis, and, second, that the the town was somewhere up the mountain that loomed darkly behind the station building. The stationmaster and his crew of four bid us warm our feet at the charcoal brazier and motioned us to wait. Finally, a young man, who introduced himself as Mike, arrived with a car.

Mike, who learned his English from U.S. soldiers in Nara, was running the forty-year-old inn for his father. As we drove up the winding, one-way road he told us about his hometown.

"Yoshino is very small," he said. "The Zaō-dō of the Kimpusen-ji temple is the second oldest building in Japan after Nara's temple. Yes, sakura still bloom, but many are gone. Last week was most beautiful. Tomorrow I'll arrange for a taxi. Sorry I cannot go with you—business in Osaka."

Jack asked, "Have you had Americans stay at your inn?"

"Yes, once," Mike replied. "Eight years ago, an army man and his family came for one week. Also, sixteen years ago, the emperor and empress stayed here. I will give you the same room."

The call of wild pheasants woke us early, and from our east-facing balcony we listened to them challenging each other from the shadowed valley. Below us the ground dropped abruptly to an echoing stream, and on the opposite mountainside the pale spring foliage of the trees contrasted with the occasional flare of a tardy sakura.

The taxi driver arrived accompanied by an eager high school student, Toshirō Shimura, who told us he spoke "just a little English." But combining our two dictionaries, we communicated very well. He had never seen Americans before and was anxious to know about life in the United States and to show us Mount Yoshino. The village is built on a mountain ridge with houses and shops facing the single street, dropping two stories at the back to overlook the valleys. Toshirō knew where the late blooming sakura were, in deep reaches of valleys where spring's warmth arrives later than on open slopes. We were a novelty to pilgrims at the shrines, and Toshirō was kept busy answering inquiries about our ages, how we liked Japan, did we have children, and telling everyone that we had come all the way from the United States to take pictures of sakura.

A petite, middle-aged lady on hanami from Kumamoto, when she learned we had been to Kumamoto ourselves, wanted to pose with us, and we in turn took pictures of her and her husband. While exchanging addresses, I noticed her sakura-printed silk bag. Pointing to cherry branches above our heads, then to the flowers on her bag, I said, "Sakura?"

"Hai, sakura." Quickly she emptied it, and pressed it into my hands, saying through Toshirō, "For a keepsake, to make a memory."

Mount Yoshino—from here it had begun—the cult of sakura. But long before language immortalized the romance of the cherry-blossom princess who married the grandson of the sun goddess, cherry trees had grown, bloomed, and died here on Yoshino, for this was the place of their origin. No sakura grew on the mainland of China or Korea. So, while the peoples of these islands through one century after another nurtured imported traditions but shaped them to their needs; absorbed foreign culture but mingled it with their own; adopted the Chinese writing system but adapted it to fit their tongues; blended religious beliefs to satisfy their souls; while wars were declared and settled—through all this, their reverence for sakura has remained uniquely their own.

Kamon ("Family crests")

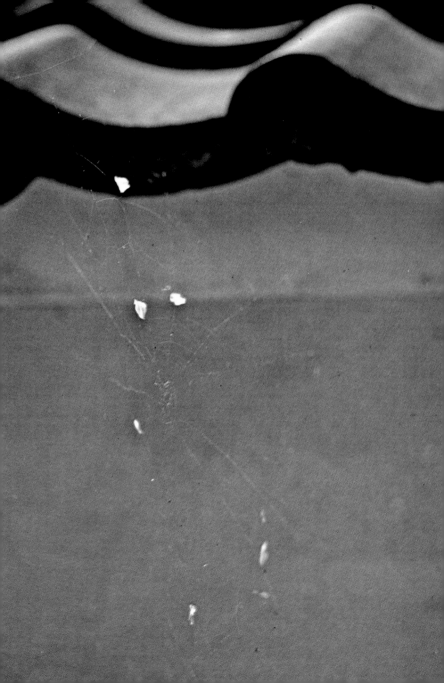

25-27. *A spider web* (*previous page*) catches falling petals at Daigo-ji temple, Kyoto, where the streamer (*left*) is flown to mark festive occasions. Below, a weeping cherry receives admiration.

29. *The shidare-zakura* blossoms in profusion and is especially splendid when the tree reaches maturity.

◄28. *Kyoto's Maruyama Park*, whose trees are lit for night viewing, is especially famous. The original weeping cherry tree was three hundred years old when it fell victim to the heat of wooden torches.

30-32. *Younger geishas* always perform the dances of the Miyako Odori, while the musicians come from the older ranks of the profession. This annual spring show, known to tourists as the "Cherry Dance," is held at the Kaburenjō theater in the Gion quarter of Kyoto.

33-36. *The five-petaled sakura design* continues to be a favorite with artists and craftsmen: left, a kimono sleeve; below left and below, cloisonné artists at work; opposite, a fan for a kabuki actor receiving its design.

37-38. *Paper lanterns and blossoms* (*left*) disappear in a short time, but the kimonoed doll (*below left*), not a plaything, may be cherished for a lifetime.

39-40. *Bonsai*, minature trees (*below and opposite*), require years of careful tending and are highly prized.

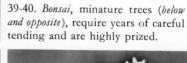

43. *Somei-yoshino,* one of hundreds of varieties of flowering cherry trees, begins to leaf out at about the time the blossoms fall.

41-42. *Blossoms* must fall, and they do so here and there at nature's bidding (*opposite and below*).

44-45. *Visitors* to the Heian Shrine in Kyoto enjoy successively cherry blossoms, iris, lotus and maple leaves, usually following a planned route through the garden.

46. *Amateur painters*, like amateur poets, are often to be seen at work in parks and gardens.

47-48. *Below* is a view across Heian Shrine's Suihō Pond. Daigoku-den (*opposite*) is a modern replica of the eighth-century Great Hall of State.

49-50. *Samurai* of another age come to life at the Cherry Blossom Festival held at Hirano Shrine, Kyoto, on the second Sunday in April.

51-54. *The costumes* in the courtly procession (*opposite and below*) are reminiscent of the early Heian period (794–898). Paraders at Hirano Shrine's festival are well adorned with cherry blossoms and the sakura design.

55. *Banners* with the sakura design often appeared on the battlefield in the days of the samurai.

56-57. *The sakura design* is everywhere: below left, as the *kamon* ("family crest") on a man's kimono; below right, on brightly colored kimono worn by girls and young ladies.

58-59. *Cherry trees* blossom in the Yamazaki Valley, south of Kyoto, although the landscape is undergoing some changes. The woman below is out blossom viewing.

60. *The somei-yoshino variety* is thought to take its name from a place on the Izu Peninsula, southwest of Tokyo.

61-63. *The tame deer* at the Kasuga Shrine in Nara are considered to be divine messengers. Souvenirs for the children may be plastic deer (*right*) or sakura-decorated wooden swords (*below right*).

64-65. *Kasuga Shrine*, standing in a quiet mountain forest, was founded in 768 by Fujiwara Nagate, great-grandson of Fujiwara Kamatari, who received the family name from the emperor. Onto a bed of moss (*below*), cherry petals and camellia have fallen together.

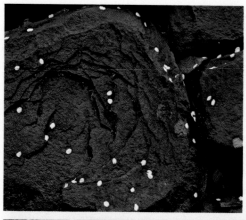

69. *The woman (overleaf)* holds a blossom that has fallen inta

66-68. Petals on the rocks, the path, stone lanterns everywhere: Kasuga Shrine has some three thousand standing and hanging lanterns.

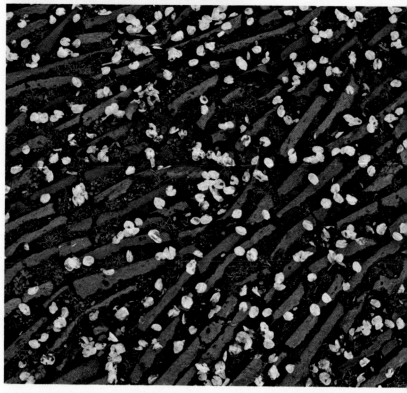

The Spirit of Sakura

"The wind's still cold, though the flowers will soon be blooming." Looking balefully at the bare, dark limbs of the cherry trees, my taxi driver in Kyoto pronounced this familiarly mournful early spring lament, for by the word "flowers" he meant, of course, Kyoto's famous cherry blossoms. Although the sakura blooms all over the country, beginning in mid-February in the furthest south and ending in northernmost Hokkaido in mid-May, for us Japanese blossoming cherry trees are at their most impressive against a traditional background, and no background so naturally fulfills that requirement as well as Kyoto, the ancient imperial capital for nearly eleven centuries, from 794, when it was founded, until 1867, the year of the Meiji Restoration, when the capital was moved to Tokyo.

For over a millennium, then, Kyoto was Japan's *miyako* (the city of the emperor), and for Kyoto's loyal citizens Tokyo's usurpation of the title is merely a temporary one: some fine day the emperor will come back and then the old city will be the *miyako* again. Thus it goes without saying that Kyoto is par excellence the site to which we Japanese make a pilgrimage to view the sakura in bloom. Of course the tree blossoms in Tokyo as well, but that is not at all the

CHERRY BLOSSOMS ✿

same thing: from 1603 until 1867, Tokyo was the capital merely of the shogunate; so much of it was destroyed during the last war (while Kyoto happily remained untouched) that it is, for all intents and purposes, a new city; and under the pressure of suddenly becoming the largest megalopolis in the world, the number of its living trees, the sakura included, is fast diminishing.

The Tokyoite who goes to Kyoto on a brief sightseeing tour will of course be impressed and charmed by the city's many ancient buildings and gardens and objects of art, but the Tokyo family that takes up residence in Kyoto will find itself not infrequently at a loss. For one thing, Tokyo people seem to be not nearly so obsessed by the weather as the people of Kyoto, and they talk about it a great deal less, listening in frank astonishment to Kyoto's constant complaints. Tokyo weather, to be sure, is not quite so capricious: summers are a little less hot and humid, winters a little less cold and damp. When winds from the Asian mainland blow over the old capital, it is gripped by cold; the next day may be fine and sunny and warm; but a day or two later the cold, dust-laden Mongolian winds will have returned. "I sweep and sweep," grumbles the Kyoto housewife, "but still everything is coated with grime. How ghastly the weather is this year!" She forgets for a moment that the weather is "ghastly" every year at this season, but then she remembers that the cold winds are only the harbingers of the true spring, when the cherry trees will burst forth in blossom. She stops her grumbling.

Another hazard the displaced Tokyo family will encounter in Kyoto is a vast number of incomprehensible local allusions, some of which are probably as old as Kyoto itself. "Have you met Miss So-and-so?" someone might ask. "She's a real Kyoto beauty

[*Kyōbijin*], but don't you feel she's just a bit like an Omuro sakura?" The Tokyoite nods uneasily and changes the subject, for he has not yet visited the famous Buddhist temple called Ninnaji in Omuro, in the western part of Kyoto. Erected originally in the ninth century, the temple is famous for its lovely five-tiered pagoda, but it is even more famous for its ancient cherry trees. Bearing multiple-petaled blossoms, the trees have short, thick trunks, with the result that the flowers are within easy reach, unlike those of taller trees. Now, the Chinese characters for "nose" and for "flower" have the same pronunciation in Japanese (*hana*): the Tokyoite will eventually come to realize that although Miss So-and-so is a great beauty, her nose is considered by some to be just a trifle flat.

Ninnaji's *yaezakura* (double-blossomed cherry trees) are visited every year at blossom time by thousands of people from all over the country. They come with their exquisitely arranged lunch boxes and their flasks of sake, bringing with them proud wooden wine cups, lacquered and so highly polished that they glisten like mirrors in the sunlight.

After lunch, some of the sakura viewers, having imbibed a bit freely, but seldom outrageously so, will start singing and dancing, for surely one in the party will have brought his samisen. The twang of the instrument will be pierced occasionally by the bamboo flutes of itinerant Zen monks. They are not beggars, these monks, but neither will they refuse alms if offered, alms that are, in turn, passed on for the further propagation of the Buddhist faith. Most of them dress very simply, wearing basket-shaped sedge hats that cover their entire heads; but now and then one sees a "monk" sporting a fine silken kimono with a gold-embroidered obi around his waist, and one suspects that he is not a monk at all. More likely he

85

CHERRY BLOSSOMS ✿

is the proprietor of one of Kyoto's many kimono shops, taking this opportunity to display the elegance of his wares. The sakura viewers admire laughingly and return to their wine and their music.

Then suddenly, with little or no warning, a heavy rain begins to fall, a rain that will strip the boughs of their blossoms. The picnickers, their merrymaking abruptly ended, hastily pack their belongings and rush to take cover under the great gate or under the eaves of the main temple, where once, in the days of Toyotomi Hideyoshi, the imperial family sought refuge. Now, while the cloudburst lasts, the temple shelters rain-soaked, shivering, considerably sobered sakura viewers; after the rainfall ends, they will make their way home beside cherry trees stripped of their blossoms. Although the flowers of Ninnaji are the longest lasting of all Kyoto's many species of sakura, their life is still a very brief one.

That very brevity, to be sure, is one of the reasons the cherry blossom exerts so strong a fascination for the Japanese, who are ever conscious of the transience of life. At the same time, the Japanese are human enough to desire to prolong the brief season. Since no one has yet acquired the ability to make a cherry blossom remain on its branch after the time has come for it to fall, store owners all over the country, in villages and towns, decorate their shops with artificial flowers as long as a month before the trees are due to blossom. The clacking and snapping of plastic flowers in the biting wind, which has now almost completely replaced the dry rustle of paper displays, seems to have become a bit of nostalgia associated with the sakura season. No matter how strong the wind, these petals do not flutter to the ground, but occasionally wire supports break and whole "branches" come flopping down.

Sensitivity toward the season permeates the most unlikely places in sometimes naive and charming ways. On side streets slightly removed from the bustle of thoroughfares dripping with plastic sakura, one finds modest houses displaying equally modest signboards: "Tea Ceremony Taught" and "Ikebana Classes Given" are written in elegant Chinese characters. Here, girls of marriageable age spend their time and their parents' money absorbing the arts of tea and flower arrangement.

In such settings, tea gatherings are often held in anticipation of the cherry blossoms. I once attended a small party where the host eschewed electric light in favor of a candlestick placed on the tatami. The flange below the candle was cut through with the design of a single cherry blossom, whose shape was waveringly projected onto the mat. Upon seeing this a guest exclaimed, "Ah, the year's first sakura!"

Even in the Ginza, the heart of the emperor's other city, the streets in early spring are decorated with paper or plastic sakura. Perhaps in Tokyo the imitation blooms are more poignant than elsewhere in the country, for there land is so expensive that few people can afford a garden and a cherry tree of their own, while at the same time Tokyo probably has fewer large public parks than any other great city in the world. And the living things in those few parks that the capital does possess are slowly being asphyxiated.

Yet if we take an elevator to the top of one of Tokyo's new skyscrapers, we discover, somewhat to our surprise, that the city is not quite so bleak as we had thought. Now, in season, we see thick clusters of pink cherry blossoms that had been invisible to us as we walked the crowded, exhaust-filled, and exhausting streets. Most of the trees are in public parks, but some still grow and bloom in private gardens. But how long, we wonder sadly and inevitably,

CHERRY BLOSSOMS ✽

will the trees continue to thrive in what has become so alien an atmosphere?

Most of Tokyo's cherry trees belong to a species called *somei-yoshino*. This is a newly developed species, relatively short-lived and not highly regarded aesthetically, but it is extremely sturdy and probably resists the damage inflicted by big-city smog better than any other species in Japan. It is also strongly resistant to insect invasion. Pale pink in color, its petals are thin and multiple and cluster thickly on the branches. At the height of its glory, it makes a brave show—too brave a show, some sakura connoisseurs feel, a show that is lacking in essential elegance.

Nonetheless, it is a tree eminently well suited to city life. It reaches full maturity in a mere twenty years, and although its life-span is not likely to exceed fifty years, it is easily replaced. Not long ago, the owner of a great restaurant transplanted some mature somei-yoshino trees into his garden and was delighted to see blossoms appear within a couple of years. The species became well known only around a century ago, but it soon became popular throughout Japan as well as in the capital. The rest of the country sees in its relatively brief life a resemblance to the people of Tokyo, who are notoriously short-tempered.

Most highly regarded, perhaps, of all species is that known as the *yamazakura*, which, as its name suggests, means "mountain cherry" or, more familiarly, "wild cherry" (*Prunus serrulata*). It has obviously been anciently cultivated in Japan, for it is frequently alluded to in the *Man'yōshū* [Collection for a myriad ages], a long anthology of poems compiled in the eighth century; the yamazakura is, however, only one of perhaps three hundred or more known varieties. In the early nineteenth century Ichihashi Nagaaki, a daimyo, produced a series of five volumes devoted exclusively to the sakura. There he listed 234 species known to him at the time. Since then the number has increased, but the yamazakura retains its title of "primus inter pares," first among equals.

The blossom has five petals, notched at the edge; the leaves are a soft, reddish brown, while the color of the petals seems to vary with the altitude at which the tree is found growing. Some blossoms are a delicate pink; others, such as those of the Nagano highlands, are nearly pure red. The latter, known as ōyamazakura, appear so deeply red against the late spring snow lingering on the mountains that viewers sometimes wonder if these are indeed cherry blossoms and not those of some less elegant tree trying to put on airs.

The yamazakura appears frequently in that favorite object of Japanese art, the picture scroll (*emakimono*), mounted on brocaded silk, which unwinds slowly to reveal the most enticing landscapes, many of them intended to depict classical Japanese scenes. The yamazakura is often shown peering through a forest of red pines, considered by ancient Japanese artists to be an appropriate background to help express the true character of the wild cherry. Generally speaking, it is only quite famous trees, such as the weeping cherries of Maruyama Park or of Heian Shrine, both in Kyoto, that are considered to possess sufficient beauty and distinction to be depicted alone, without a background of other trees, on picture scrolls.

One famous *emakimono* shows the Buddhist priest Saigyō, who was also a well-known poet, climbing the rocky slopes of Mount Yoshino in search of the yamazakura, whose petals there were every bit as red as those of Nagano. Set against the still snow-

CHERRY BLOSSOMS ✿

capped peaks and the deep blue pools of melted snow, the scene is one of exquisite beauty, similar to that of ancient Nagano: the "Saigyō Emaki," as the scroll is called, takes us straight back to the twelfth century. Some say that the poet-priest, in seeking the yamazakura of Yoshino, was in fact hoping to attain satori, the enlightenment that is the ultimate goal of Buddhism.

One of the most attractive places in all Japan to view the yamazakura is the old Shūzan road, across which, in ancient times, fresh fish preserved in salt were brought from Wakasa Bay to the imperial capital in Kyoto. The road winds through a valley shaded on both sides by thousands of Kitayama cedars, which are used as pillars in the most elegant Japanese homes. The cedars are made to grow straight, with bare trunks, displaying leaves only at the crown, for they are as carefully cultivated as rare flowers in a garden; when branches begin to appear, they are removed, and the tree is carefully bound so that it will rise as clean as a stone column. This vast forest of living pillars is a magnificent sight, a magnificence that is enhanced in springtime by the deep glowing red of the wild cherry.

If we continue along the Shūzan road, we eventually reach the Buddhist temple called Jōjōji, where once, during a troubled time in Japanese history, a former emperor served as a priest and where now people make the long pilgrimage in order to view its famous giant weeping cherry towering above a stretch of immaculate white sand. The temple itself, although of ancient foundation, has been recently reconstructed and is not especially interesting.

But the tree itself, a *shidare-zakura* (weeping or drooping cherry), is huge and beautiful and old beyond memory. Its great branches spread forth in all directions, and for nearly a week in blossom time, depending on the weather, it is a sight of staggering splendor, especially in the golden rays of the morning or evening sun. Then, after a time, like the gentle rain from heaven, the blossoms begin to drift slowly down onto the sand beneath, pale pink raindrops that linger for a moment on the pure white floor.

Jōjōji's priests are very much aware of the austere and immemorial beauty of their weeping cherry; they restrict viewing to a mere few hours during the week, and they permit no frivolity in its presence. Before the front gate stands a stone slab engraved with the admonition: "Alcoholic beverages and meat and vegetables that stink [garlic] are prohibited." Once upon a time that word "meat" included women, but Jōjōji has bowed to the pressure of twentieth-century liberalization and now permits female viewers, although it still maintains its other prohibitions. When I visited the temple, I heard a man mutter to a companion that he wished he had a flask of sake with him; he was promptly evicted by a priest who had overheard the same intemperate remark. Nor is it considered correct to speak in a voice loud enough to be heard by strangers nearby; visitors are expected to whisper their words of pleasure at viewing the famous tree.

This careful reticence is very unlike what happens at blossom-viewing time in Tokyo, where huge throngs converge on Ueno Park, bringing with them their food and sake and samisens. Lining the paths of the park at viewing time are open-air stalls, past which drunken revelers, singing and shouting, thread their precarious way. One has the feeling that the crowds have come to Ueno with the object of having a bit of fun rather than merely paying homage to the transient and venerated blossom.

The assumption would pretty much be right. Formerly the park boasted a handsome forest of somei-yoshino trees, but during the harsh wartime and increasingly polluted postwar years the trees have dwindled, peaked, and pined to the point where they hardly seem worth the trouble of taking the elevated train to Ueno unless the visitor is well fortified with food and wine and good company. Originally the estate of a daimyo and then the site of a Buddhist temple under the patronage of the shogun, Ueno was the scene of a bloody battle between the shogun's army and the forces loyal to the emperor, a battle that the shogun lost, as he was destined to lose the civil war itself, after which he acceded to imperial restoration in 1867.

In the course of the one-day Ueno battle, the temple was destroyed. Then, after Emperor Meiji moved to Tokyo, Ueno was converted into a public park, in which are located several important museums, and a great many trees were planted in the torn and stained ground, including a cypress and a magnolia planted by General Ulysses S. Grant and his wife on a visit to Japan in 1879, and of course a vast number of cherry trees, many of them on a small plateau called Sakuragaoka (Cherry Hill). Now there are far fewer than there were, and those that remain seem rather forlorn: the trunks are dusty, and the blossoms glow pink for only the briefest while before they too are dimmed by dust. It is not a happy sight for a sober sakura lover; he must go elsewhere if he would quench his thirst.

One place he might try is Kyoto's Kiyomizudera, a temple founded originally at the end of the eighth century and one of the imperial capital's two most popular sakura-viewing sites. Kiyomizu will, quite naturally, be crowded in blossom time, but the flower-viewing parties are sedate, and drunken revelers are a great deal fewer and farther between than in Tokyo. Many of the trees are, as in Ueno, the familiar somei-yoshino, but Kiyomizu also boasts a wooden platform overlooking a deep cliff, on the opposite side of which grows the more dramatic and beautiful yamazakura amid a forest of maples and pines.

The deep valley of Kiyomizu is famous throughout the country and has given rise to a familiar proverbial Japanese expression. A man who has figuratively jumped down into Kiyomizu's gorge has summoned together all the courage he possesses, he has burnt his bridges, he has crossed his Rubicon: his decision made, he is prepared to accept its consequences, whatever they may be.

Kiyomizu also appears in nō drama in a play called *Tamura*. Here a priest, having come to view the cherry blossoms, chances suddenly upon a young lad of whom he inquires about the origins of the temple. The boy replies that it was founded by the famous General Sakanoue-no-Tamuramaro, who dedicated it in gratitude to the Eleven-faced Kannon (one of the manifestations of the Goddess of Mercy). The priest then asks the boy his name, and the boy answers, "Just watch where I go." With that he disappears into the Tamurado (the chapel of the general) on a hill behind the temple, and the priest realizes that the boy can be none other than the ghost of the young Sakanoue-no-Tamuramaro himself. As the play continues, the priest at one point sings a song in which he compares the mists and clouds about him to the pure white cherry blossoms. Such blossoms are truly appropriate to the miyako, the city of the emperor. The austere nō stage is almost never decorated with bright, flowering cherry branches, but the song of the priest evokes the familiar and well-loved sight in the minds of the audience more vividly than any real boughs could do.

Kyoto's other popular cherry-viewing site is Maruyama, twenty-

CHERRY BLOSSOMS ✽

one acres of handsome landscape gardening that constitute the old imperial capital's chief public park. It lies close to Yasaka Shrine, more commonly known as Gion Shrine, and gives its name to the city's most famous festival, which dates back to the year 876, when the head priest of the shrine led a procession to supplicate divine intervention against a plague that was ravaging the city. Plagues are unknown in Kyoto now, but the procession still continues, probably the most splendid, and certainly the most famous, in the whole country. Although it takes place in the overpowering heat of July, Kyotoites choose to ignore the discomfort: each family displays in open windows and doorways its finest screens and brocades, so that the city seems like one gigantic art museum, and everywhere the sound of the festival music, the Gion *bayashi*, is to be heard.

Blossom time at Maruyama, called Gion no Yozakura ("Night-sakura" of Gion), occurs happily at an earlier and cooler time of year. The park possesses a tremendous number of different species of cherry, which, when they are in bloom, are artificially illuminated at night. Naturally enough, the sight attracts many thousands of viewers who come to eat and drink and sing and dance as well as admire the blossoms; but, as always in Kyoto, the crowds are far more decorous than those of brash, young, bustling Tokyo.

One sight no one wants to miss is Maruyama's giant weeping cherry, which, when lighted at night by pine torches, looks like a great fountain shooting its pale delicate blossoms into the dark night sky. It was, in fact, those very torches that contributed to the death of the original tree, generally considered at the time an ominous tragedy; happily, however, the weeping cherry that was planted in its place grew to maturity far more quickly than was expected, and now its blossoms are thought to be as fine as those of its doomed predecessor.

The blossoming of the new tree is taken to be the culminating point of Kyoto's springtide, and everyone who comes to view the sight sniffs anxiously at the weather, for wind and rain will put an untimely end to the blossoms. Then the ground will be thick with them, as though covered by a heavy snowfall. This is not a mere fanciful allusion, for the falling of the blossoms is called *hana fubuki* ("a storm of falling blossoms"); each year we hope it will not come prematurely, although we know, the moment the trees burst into bloom, that the "storm" is already on its way. It is a glorious sight to view the short-lived blossoms and sad to say farewell to them, sad but inevitable; no man knows whether he will be here to admire them again when spring returns.

The Gion quarter, which stretches from Maruyama Park to Shijō Bridge, is famous for its many teahouses and other places of amusement as well as for the theater called Kaburenjō where, every year between the first of April and mid-May, the Miyako Odori is performed. The visiting foreigner generally refers to it as the "Cherry Dance," although in fact the Japanese words mean no more than "the dance of the imperial city." However, the "Cherry Dance" is an adequately descriptive name, for despite the fact that there are scenes representing all four seasons, the performance takes place during cherry-blossom time, and the dance devoted to the sakura is the climax. Although the Miyako Odori is not of ancient origin, it has, since 1872, been an integral part of Kyoto's spring festivities. Residents of the district have little hesitation in claiming that Kyoto's cherry trees do not bloom because spring has come but rather because the Miyako Odori is being performed.

CHERRY BLOSSOMS ✱

The dancing girls, or *maiko*, wear the most gorgeous brocaded and embroidered kimonos, with long and fabulously beautiful obis to match. Discussing money matters in connection with maiko is considered the height of bad taste, but it might be observed here, parenthetically of course, that kimono and obi together frequently cost a million yen or more, over three thousand dollars at the rate of exchange prevailing at this instant of writing. The coiffure of the girls is as ornamental as their dress, and spectators often wonder how they manage to keep such elaborate hairdos in place as they dance. One answer is that their faces are so heavily painted with thick white pigment that they are quite incapable of expressing emotion. The heads of the maiko, thus, remain fairly rigid, and the meaning of the dance must be conveyed in other ways, through the pulling of a sleeve, perhaps, or the manipulation of the ever-present fan.

Much of the music is supplied by geishas kneeling stage right and left, where they play the samisen and sing the songs; from time to time they are joined by a flutist. During the hour-long performance, there are eight quick scene changes, including plum trees in blossom within a shrine garden, the planting of rice at the foot of a mountain, a rain shower at a famous place, a flaming forest of red maples, a snow scene, and finally the climax: a stage full of blossoming sakura. Now the fan of the maiko is painted in a cherry-blossom pattern, and her kimono too is richly decorated with the same stylized blossom. On one cheek she wears a small bouquet of cherry flowers.

Once the last performance of the day is ended, the dancers hurry off through a dense crowd of admirers to their evening jobs, jobs that consist of pouring out drinks for clients who have taken a large private room in an expensive restaurant, then dancing and singing for them. No more than that is to be expected: the maiko are far too busy, far too professional to be anything but distressingly respectable.

At the western edge of Kyoto, beside the Ōi River, lies Arashiyama, long considered to be the quintessence of scenic beauty. Lady Murasaki, who speaks of it as the loveliest place in Japan, has her hero, Genji, attempt to reconstruct it in his private garden. Arashiyama is especially noted for its maples and its cherry trees; in blossom time, in fact, the latter burst forth in such profusion that from a distance the hill of Arashiyama looks as though it is veiled in white mist.

One sakura story that centers around Arashiyama is irresistible. The time is the so-called Golden Age of the Tokugawa shogunate (the end of the seventeenth century), and the hero is one Kōrin, of the Ogata family. Kōrin's father, a noted connoisseur of Japanese swords and a relative of Hon'ami Kōetsu, one of the greatest figures in Japanese art history, was the proprietor of a textile shop so eminent that it supplied kimonos for both the consort of the emperor and the mistress of the shogun; Kōrin's brother Kenzan was a well-known maker of ceramics, and a poet and painter as well; but despite all these artistic connections Kōrin himself, during his youth, led a life of idleness and dissipation. One day, however, he discovered that he was possessed of a rare artistic talent, and so he apprenticed himself to a well-known artist. His efforts rewarded, he became famous throughout the country as a designer of *makie* (gold- or silver-lacquered scenes on boxes), which soon commanded the highest prices.

During blossom time, it was the custom for well-to-do families of Kyoto to betake themselves, in their finest clothes, to Arashi-yama to view the cherry trees, each family bringing its lunch in an expensive box embellished with *makie*. One day Kōrin appeared, wearing not the expected elaborate kimono but rather one of the most ordinary kind. General astonishment only increased when it was seen that his lunch was not carefully arranged in a decorated box but was merely wrapped in bamboo bark; then, as he undid the bark, everyone, by now both bewildered and fascinated, observed that it contained only a few rice balls, the food of the poorest working man.

Unconcernedly, Kōrin munched his rice balls, but as they disappeared the absorbed onlookers saw that painted on the bark was a gorgeous makie depicting pure golden cherry trees in bloom. Clearly the makie was worth a fortune! Seeing that he had everyone's attention, Kōrin laughed. "It is mortifying," he said, "for ladies and gentlemen such as yourselves to be confronted with such grossly inferior work." With that, he crumpled the bark and tossed it casually into the swiftly flowing river.

Had Kōrin not destroyed the bit of bamboo before he threw it into the water, he might have put some petals on it and transformed it into a miniature *hana ikada*. At Arashiyama, the river is known as the Ōi, but further upstream it is called the Hozu, and as it descends from the mountains, where it has its source, to Kyoto, it dashes through a series of rapids. Logs for timber were customarily lashed together into rafts in hillside forests and floated downriver; when the sakura was in bloom, these rafts were decorated with flowering cherry branches for the pleasure of riverside viewers. The floats, called *hana ikada* ("flower rafts"), soon became the basis for one of Japan's most popular sakura designs. The cherry-raft theme was, and still is, used not only on kimonos and obis but also on many other decorated objects.

One such is the fan. I remember paying a visit to Kyoto's best-known fan maker, Kiyoe Nakamura. It was a cold day, even though the cherries were already in blossom, one of those times we call *hanabie* ("flower-cold"), yet despite the inclement weather, Nakamura's sliding doors were half open, and he himself lay sound asleep on the tatami, snoring loudly. Knowing him to be rather partial to the bottle and fearing that he might catch cold lying there uncovered, I shook him awake. He looked up blearily for a moment, then recognized me and offered his apologies. I, in turn, apologized for waking him.

All about lay a profuse litter of various kinds of paper, the paper on which he painted his famous fans. Rummaging about, he eventually found what he was looking for; it was a sheet of hand-made paper of the finest quality, the kind that is customarily reserved for the writing of presentation poems. On it Nakamura had painted a hana ikada, the cherry blossoms glistening a pale pearly white. "I was just having a bit of fun," Nakamura muttered offhandedly.

It was a lovely piece of work. "Would you consider selling it to me?" I asked.

He seemed a bit embarrassed. "Actually," he replied, "it was for an order I got from the master of the Senke tea-ceremony school. But since it's turned out so well, I don't really want to sell it. I shall give it to you," he added impulsively.

"But what about your order?" I asked, reluctant to accept his quixotic gift.

He laughed. "The Senke master," he said finally, "is always complaining that though my work is excellent and my character too is excellent, I am incorrigibly and hopelessly lazy. I shall merely give him further proof! The hana ikada is yours."

The master of Senke, for whom the work had been specially done, held an extremely high position in the world of the Japanese tea ceremony; I felt it would be impossibly churlish on my part to refuse the gift a second time, and that is how I came into possession of one of my favorite sakura paintings.

Nakamura himself, although he chooses to work amid a squalid jumble of paper in a dusty room, is an eminent and highly successful artist, and he is also a very learned connoisseur. Behind him, where he had lain sleeping, I saw a pair of lovely screens of the Kamakura period decorated in an elaborate fan design, while on a nearby shelf, inch deep in dust, stood a tiny sixteenth-century Buddha of fabulous craftsmanship. His own designs, so vital and original when he creates them, frequently achieve such popularity that one sees them copied (in a debased form) everywhere, even in certain expensive restaurants, whose cooks will arrange plates of food in accordance with Nakamura's designs.

Another contemporary who must never be omitted from any account, however brief, of Japanese cherry blossoms is Shintarō Sasabe of Osaka. The son of a well-to-do but rather eccentric father, he was told as a boy that he might spend as much money as he liked on his education but that he was never to use that education as a means to commercial or financial success. "What good is learning," his father would ask, "if success is its only object?" Then he would add: "A man must never be afraid to say what he really thinks. Salaried men, with their eyes on some material goal, are inevitably cowards." The young Sasabe, following his father's well-meant advice and taking advantage of the family wealth, has devoted a large part of his life to the study and cultivation of the sakura; he has become its foremost exponent and defender.

A graduate of the law school of the University of Tokyo, he preferred the cherry tree to jurisprudence and in a suburb of Osaka created an enormous sakura forest, where he set about the laborious process of elaborating new species. The somei-yoshino, which seemed to be taking over the entire country, he despised as the least beautiful of all species. While quietly pursuing his horticultural goals, he suddenly found himself engulfed in a war, a desperate war for the pursuit of which the sakura was the source not of lovely, short-lived and poignant blossoms but of much-needed timber. In his book, *Sakuraotoko Gyōjōki* [My life and cherry], he writes: "My beloved cherry trees, as dear to me as my own family, were just about to mature. When I saw hundreds of them being mercilessly cut down, my angry heart felt as though it was about to burst within me." Despite the wood-hungry prefectural government, despite even the all-powerful imperial army, Sasabe continued to fight on. He toured the nation speaking in defense of the sakura. But who, in a country that was hopelessly waging a catastrophic war, was disposed to listen? Some merely ignored him, others openly derided him. Dispirited, Sasabe retired to his Osaka forest and there, alone, he went on trying to produce superior saplings by means of grafting.

Then, unexpectedly, he found help. It came in the form of a gardener who was highly experienced in the art of grafting and who also had been ignored or dismissed by the military establishment. His name was Hikotarō Hirao, and at first, according to Sasabe, he was very reluctant to divulge the secrets of his craft, but at last he was won over. Together, the two men worked on while the war raged about them and above them. In their self-appointed task of evolving finer strains of sakura, they were greatly aided by the fact that Hirao possessed a set of gardening and grafting tools fashioned by Chiyozuru Korehide, a famous sword maker. Each tool was in itself a work of art. Hirao's death, during the midst of the war, was mourned by none save Sasabe, to whom the lovely tools made by Chiyozuru were bequeathed, as well as a good bit of the sakura lore and the green thumb that Hirao had acquired.

Sasabe continued, and continues still, his work, but he is none too optimistic about it. He does not foresee a happy future for the sakura, and one reason, he says, is that Japanese botanists pay more attention to the classification of trees than to the creation of new species or the preservation of old ones. Not a single example of the country's most famous cherry trees, according to Sasabe, is in healthy condition.

As a case in point he cites the story of the great tree of Gifu Prefecture, which is estimated to be some thirteen hundred years old, with tremendous branches spreading as wide as 150 feet. Back in 1926, the tree had already begun visibly to weaken because of the great number of parasite trees that had taken hold of its branches. In discussions as to how the sakura might be saved, many dendrologists suggested that the parasites be removed, but Sasabe replied that such an operation would only weaken the tree still further. He said that a younger tree should have been grafted onto the old tree while it was still strong, but this essential step had not been taken; and now, Sasabe concluded mournfully, the time to take it had passed.

Further, he tells the history of Maruyama's giant weeping cherry, transplanted from Gion Shrine in 1820 to another temple and then transplanted again to the center of the park. After it became famous throughout the country as the Gion no Yozakura, that fame was destined to be its death, for in blossom time crowds came with lighted torches, and the alternate heating and cooling of the surrounding air weakened the tree. When Sasabe was asked how it might be saved, he replied that the only way he knew was to ask Hikotarō Hirao, then living in Tokyo, to graft new roots onto the roots of the old tree. But the people of Kyoto declared vehemently that it went against the grain to ask a Tokyoite to come to the salvation of a Kyoto tree. And so Japan's most famous sakura was left to die.

Despite his disillusionment, however, Sasabe has not given up all hope. When asked to describe what he believes to be the ideal sakura, he replies: the sapling must attain maturity quickly; the tree must be able to withstand extremes of temperature; it must blossom regularly at the same time of year, and the blossoms must be graceful in form; the color and shape of the young leaves must be good; and the tree must possess within itself the ability eventually to grow into a giant. Despite the stringency of his requirements, Sasabe continues to experiment in the hope of someday combining them all in a single new species.

It would not be proper to conclude an essay on the sakura without saying a word or two about the profound influence it has exerted upon the art, the artifacts and the daily life of the Japanese people. It is, more than any other, our national flower; and that wartime American book about Japan, *The Chrysanthemum and the Sword*, ought perhaps more accurately to have been called "The Cherry Blossom and the Sword," for the chrysanthemum, although it is the symbol of the imperial family, does not occupy the place in Japanese hearts and minds and eyes that is given to the cherry blossom.

In the theatrical arts, for example, nō is not the only form of drama that makes use of the sakura. Kabuki, although it began in Kyoto in the early sixteenth century, soon moved to Tokyo (then called Edo), where it began to enjoy an enormous popularity with the burgeoning class of townsfolk, for whom the sakura became, indeed, the symbol of kabuki. It also, incidentally, became a symbol for the expensive courtesans of Yoshiwara, a licensed quarter near present-day Asakusa, which is also an amusement center. The *oiran* of Yoshiwara, as they were called, were known as "flowers"; they enjoyed a high reputation in the city, and it was no rare sight to see a well-to-do merchant bringing his young unmarried sons to Yoshiwara to be initiated by highly skilled professionals into the rites of sex. The flowers of Yoshiwara, even later when much of Europe and America was gripped by Victorian hypocrisy, were not thought of as "fallen women": on the contrary, they were handsome and beautifully costumed charmers pursuing an ancient, respectable and perhaps necessary vocation.

At least one of Yoshiwara's *oiran* is the heroine of a kabuki drama, *Sukeroku Yukari no Edo-zakura* [Sukeroku Yukari, the playboy of old Edo]. It is not, in all truth, a very good play, even by the most melodramatic kabuki standards, but it captures the imagination of the theatergoing public, in part because of its elegant music, its graceful dances, and its elaborate stage settings, all of them related to the cherry blossom. The rather simple, triangular plot concerns a beautiful courtesan of Yoshiwara and two men who were rivals for her affections, one of them wholly unscrupulous and always sumptuously dressed, the other quite honest but given to a simple black silk kimono with an ordinary bamboo flute tucked into his obi. All three, the girl and the two aspirants for her love, were symbols of Edo's cherry blossoms, thus giving the play its title, and, as such, they fascinate the audience. Some profess to see in the play a denunciation of the samurai class and a resistance to its overweening power by merchants and artisans, but in all likelihood it was the sakura sumptuousness of the dress and decor that made a more direct and immediate appeal.

In the graphic arts of Japan, the sakura, as we have already noted, has long played a highly important role, and continues to do so. Two modern artists who must be mentioned in this connection are Taikan Yokoyama and Meiji Hashimoto. It was the former who took as his inspiration for one of the finest of all sakura paintings Maruyama's famous weeping cherry. This was the original tree, painted before its unfortunate death, and virtually the entire canvas is devoted to its lovely blossoms. Only a small bit of the night sky may be seen in the background, with smoke rising from flaming torches. This is considered by many to be Taikan's finest work, and since it is a painting of our own time it has an immediacy for us that some older sakura pictures lack.

Another recent sakura painting was done for Tokyo's new imperial palace, built in 1969 to replace the old one destroyed in the air raid of May 26, 1945. Here modern as well as traditional methods of architecture were used, and the builders, architects, painters, decorators and gardeners were given freer rein than ever before in the construction of an imperial building. Hashimoto chose to paint a yaezakura on one of the corridor walls of the main palace.

He began by traveling about the country, sketching a great

many trees, and finally settled on the well-known *takizakura* ("water-fall cherry," from the shape of the tree of Fukushima Prefecture). He not only sketched the 650-year-old tree in the glory of full bloom but also returned to it during the winter to examine its bare boughs, much as earlier painters of the West studied human skeletons in order to lend verisimilitude to their crucifixions and their pietàs. The result of Hashimoto's labors is a sakura wall-painting of extraordinary beauty.

Far earlier in time are the picture scrolls (*emakimono*), devoted to the sakura, which we have already noted. Many of these were produced during the four-century-long Heian period, a period that began at the end of the eighth century when Emperor Kammu established his capital at Kyoto and that for all practical purposes came to a close when the shogun's government was established at Kamakura. The Heian artistic climax may be thought of as having been attained around the time of Lady Murasaki's *Genji Monogatari*. It was a period of great elegance that saw the glorification of the quiet restraint still so highly regarded in Japanese art.

Since it relates a coherent story through a series of scenes, the emakimono was never intended to be viewed at a single glance but rather was to be enjoyed slowly as it was unrolled. The cherry tree generally employed in older emakimono is the rather slow-blooming yamazakura, with its red-tinted leaves (the quick-blooming somei-yoshino did not exist at the time); such a picture scroll often showed various stages in the flowering process of the yamazakura.

Except for extremely famous trees, the sakura was seldom depicted in isolation. It was usually surrounded by other trees, or else it was part of what are called "human-interest scenes," which

70. *A boy* in Tokyo shows that the enjoyment of sakura begins at a young age.

71-75. *Shinjuku Imperial Garden* in central Tokyo is extremely popular for school excursions (*previous page and opposite*). The *satozakura* (*left*) is the species given by the people of Tokyo to the people of Washington, D. C., in 1912.

76-78. *Flower-viewing time* may be the occasion for any number of divertissements. The combo practicing above is made up of university students.

79-81. *One variety* of satozakura (*right*) is pink. Below, a group photo is a natural part of a school excursion to Shinjuku Imperial Garden.

82. *Shogetsu* is another variety of sato-zakura, which, unlike the *yamazakura* and *higan* varieties, is a hybrid produced by man.

83. *A flower arrangement* reflects the season; the teacher belongs to the Ikenobō school, which has many overseas branches.

84. *The young lady's kimono* brings to mind that worn in kabuki drama.

85-86. *Toys, and the blossom* itself reflected—encounters with sakura come about in many ways.

87-89. *Omiya Park*, in the suburbs of Tokyo, is one of many smaller parks whose quietness attracts people of all ages (*opposite and overleaf*), and, of course, Sunday painters on any day of the week (*below*).

often included stylized renderings of farm houses. It must be noted here that rural dwellings in Japan are not built to protect or isolate man from nature but rather to harmonize the two. Nature is never regarded as an antagonist but instead as an ever-present force to which man gladly adapts himself. This point of view finds eloquent expression in the ancient emakimono, where, for example, a farm might be depicted with its roof removed, so that the interior is visible. Realism discarded, man is shown to be so thoroughly at one with nature that he no longer requires even a roof to his house. Nor, in an attempt to achieve that same harmony, is the depiction of the sakura, with a fleecy cloud floating above it, entirely realistic.

Most of the pigments used in early emakimono were of mineral origin, and the colors are therefore long-lasting, but the pigments themselves were liable to flake off with the frequent rolling and unrolling of the scrolls. For that reason, the finest of the old emaki-mono, such as the *Genji Monogatari Emaki*, a National Treasure, are generally now exhibited unrolled and beneath long sheets of glass, within a carefully controlled atmosphere.

After Buddhism was introduced into Japan from Korea in the sixth century, the copying of sutras onto fine quality paper came to be considered an artistic experience as well as an act of piety. It is interesting to note that many such early copies of the sutras are decorated with drawings and paintings of the cherry blossom, so that these too contribute to our knowledge of the way in which our ancestors viewed the sakura—as an object of reverence and beauty, the symbol of a well-lived life, however brief.

Moving onward in the history of Japanese art, we come to the very short Momoyama period (end of the sixteenth century and beginning of the seventeenth), during which Toyotomi Hideyoshi, a peasant who began his extraordinary career as a groom to the warrior Nobunaga, succeeded eventually in wresting from the imperial court the title of Kwampaku, which made him both civil and military master of almost all of Japan. Over and above the remarkable talents that lifted him to this eminence, Hideyoshi was an enthusiastic connoisseur of the arts and a devotee of the sakura. He is as famous in Japanese history for his blossom-viewing parties as for his military sorties.

There are still in existence a number of painted screens (*byōbue*) as well as easel paintings of the genre type, both of the Momoyama period, depicting the viewing of cherry blossoms in Daigo, a suburb of Kyoto, and Yoshino. The sakura was frequently used also, during the same brief Momoyama era, in domestic decoration on interior walls and on sliding doors (*fusuma*). Characteristic of such paintings is that showing the yaezakura of Chishakuin temple, in Kyoto, its red blossoms set off by the green of cedars and willows, all against a background of golden clouds.

After the death of Hideyori, Hideyoshi's son and successor, who committed suicide in 1615 following a military defeat, came the rise of the Tokugawas. With Ieyasu entrenched as the first Tokugawa shogun, there began a period of intense building of temples, shrines and castles; and the painters who were chosen to decorate the new buildings were mostly members of the Kanō school, which had flourished both before and during the Momoyama period, and which continued to make eloquent and frequent use of the sakura as a decorative theme.

The same is true of Japan's traditional applied arts, although present-day connoisseurs and collectors resent that restrictive adjective "applied," for many of these objects, despite the very practical use for which they were originally produced, are true works of art in themselves. Take, for example, ancient Japanese implements of war such as swords and armor, both now famous throughout the world, both fetching exceptionally high prices at auctions in London, Paris, and New York, and both to be seen carefully enclosed within glass cases in the world's museums.

As far back as the thirteenth century, expert Japanese sword makers had begun to achieve a personal fame that was denied their fellow craftsmen in most other countries of the world. After a master had produced a sword for a member of the samurai class entitled to possess it, the latter would, on his death, pass it on to his son as one of his most treasured legacies. It was a work of art, it was a status symbol, and it was also, as it was intended to be, a killer. Sir Ernest Satow, who spent twenty-five years in Japan both before and after the imperial restoration, describes in his book *A Diplomat in Japan* his great astonishment at the unbelievable sharpness of samurai swords.

Perhaps for that very reason, sword guards at the base of the hilt were considered to be highly important, and a well-to-do samurai might possess as many as fifty guards for the same sword, using whichever seemed to him most suitable to the occasion. The scabbard too was of course an essential adjunct, and the entire ensemble (blade, guard, hilt, scabbard) was intricately decorated, often with a sakura design, for the short-lived blossom was especially dear to the samurai, who never knew from one moment to the next when he might find himself engaged in a battle to the death or when he might be required by his strict code to commit ritual suicide. The finest hilts, made of iron, would be inlaid with a sakura pattern in either gold or silver or perhaps both.

CHERRY BLOSSOMS ✿

Ancient Japanese armor, splendid and varied as it was, came to be considered a treasured work of art only after it fell into disuse in actual battle. For many centuries, that armor was put to a practical purpose, and each type of helmet and each suit of mail had its own name, depending on the way in which it was produced, the way the mail was sewn together by silken threads, the way the leathern part of the armor was dyed. This plate armor was usually inlaid with elaborate designs in gold or silver and was also elegantly tinted to resemble the colors used by women in their *kasane* (heavy garments worn over the kimono in cold weather). Just as the women possessed sakura *kasane*, so warriors used plate armor of a similar theme called *kozakura odoshi*, the name deriving from "small cherry" designs on the leather "braid" that joined the plates together. Itsukushima Shrine possesses a particularly fine and well-known example.

For many centuries, Japanese warfare followed immutable rules of etiquette, from which it would have been unthinkable for a samurai to deviate. One such rule required that a combatant before encountering the foe shout out his name, his rank and his military history as well as, on occasion, that of his ancestors if it was thought sufficiently illustrious to have a discouraging effect on the enemy. But in 1281 Japan was invaded by Mongols who did not quite ignore the samurai as he valiantly proclaimed his name and lineage: they simply filled him full of poisoned arrows, a method of warfare despised by the Japanese, or else they surrounded him and leisurely cut him to pieces. They also, apparently, possessed gunpowder, which they had brought with them from the Asian mainland.

Although a sudden typhoon scattered the Mongol horde, giving victory of a sort to the Japanese, it was by now apparent to the samurai that their traditional armor and their traditional means of waging war were inadequate to cope with the changing world of the thirteenth century. As the old suits of mail began to be replaced on the battlefield, they found their way into family treasuries: they became works of art. Indeed, once they were no longer put to practical use, they were considered so beautiful that they were employed as themes for emakimono and other types of painting.

Another of Japan's "applied" arts that has elevated itself to the rank of "pure" art is pottery. Japan is a land where ceramics are deeply loved and wholeheartedly appreciated. Kilns, dating from the earliest times onward, have been found in virtually every part of the country, and potters have produced innumerable objects of stoneware, earthenware and porcelain, many of them, like swords and armor, to be found now in private collections or public museums. The cherry blossom, inevitably, became one of the potters' commonest decorative themes, although the most famous tea masters tended to regard the sakura as a bit too colorful for tea bowls themselves. With the alliance between the tea cult and Zen Buddhism, it was considered essential that tea utensils should be austere and restrained, as should the decor of the room itself (*shibui* is the Japanese word), and cherry blossoms were not generally considered to fulfill this decorative ideal. However, many other great and beautiful pieces of Japanese pottery do make good use of the blossoming sakura.

Indeed, nowhere else in the world does this decorative theme enter so pervasively into the daily life of the people, although we must admit that once it was more frequently encountered than it is now when traditional handicraft tends to be increasingly replaced by mass production. Where the craftsman's hands cannot feasibly be supplanted by the machine, the art or craft is likely to die out. There is, for example, in Japan today only one true master in the use of inlaid mother-of-pearl, where once, in ages past, there were many such artists. The Shōsōin Repository, in Nara, contains a vast array of objects that once belonged to Emperor Shōmu (724– 49) and that were presented to Todai-ji temple by his consort after his death. There the visitor may see many fine examples of nacre work (called *raden*), of which a number make use of the sakura theme, offering eloquent proof that once upon a time in Japan *raden* was a highly regarded art and one that craftsmen were content to spend many years learning.

The inlaying of the shimmering, iridescent bits of mother-of-pearl into lacquer and applying lacquer around them is an extremely complex and difficult skill to acquire, necessitating a long apprenticeship. Yet from the beginning of the Heian period through the end of the Edo period, the skill was used to decorate many precious objects of daily use, such as bookshelves or boxes to contain the fine paper on which poems were to be written. Today, Japan's single great raden master is Tatsuaki Kuroda, who created the great decorative tray for the new imperial palace.

Indeed, all hand-polished lacquerwork, not only that involving the use of mother-of-pearl, has fallen upon sad times in modern industrialized Japan. There are, at present, only a few craftsmen producing lacquer ware of the finest quality, where once it was a commonly acquired skill, for ordinary soup bowls were hand-lacquered and polished to provide a protective and insulating surface for the hot liquid. Generally, the interior of the bowls was left undecorated, but the exterior was often painted in a sakura design.

❋ THE SPIRIT OF SAKURA

Hand-woven and embroidered textiles, such as the famous Nishijin brocade of Kyoto or the figured brocade called *tsuzure-nishiki*, have fared somewhat better, largely perhaps because the female of the species, in Japan as elsewhere in the world, likes to wear the most interesting clothes she can find. And in Japan, despite its growing westernization, the most interesting garments are still considered to be the traditional ones. A bride, for example, may be married in a Christian or Christian-type ceremony, wearing white as in the West, but when she appears at the traditional reception that follows the ceremony she will wear a gorgeous kimono and obi, frequently embroidered in gold in (if the season is right) one or another of Japan's many sakura themes.

Recently I discussed this matter with the proprietor of a shop that specializes in the weaving of obis of Nishijin brocade, such as those worn by the maiko of Gion. He told me that because of the elaborate handwork involved, the use of the sakura pattern has become less common than it once was, for the obis are now enormously expensive, and an obi based on a sakura theme may properly be worn only during that brief time when the cherry trees are in bloom. Designs that may be used throughout the year, he said, have become more usual, but he added quickly that so long as Japanese women continue to wear kimonos, the sakura theme will continue to be employed, for no other decorative element is so throughly, so typically, and so uniquely Japanese.

Nor is the male of the species any more immune to the spell of the blossom; he finds it on his cigarette cases, his pipes and tobacco boxes, his tie pins and cuff links: it is a recurrent pattern in his life as well as in his wife's. And it is a recurrent pattern also in every Japanese household. Even in a lonely mountain cottage

CHERRY BLOSSOMS ✻

or a remote farmhouse, the sakura appears and reappears, often as a stopgap or emergency measure. Japanese houses still use, as they have for centuries, sliding doors made of paper on a wooden frame (called *shōji*). Obviously, these are fragile objects not intended to last forever, nor to withstand a careless childish elbow. However, it is a time-consuming task to remove all the torn paper and paste on a whole new sheet, so until that becomes necessary, the housewife is likely to cut out bits of paper in the five-petaled sakura design and past them over the holes. This is a very ancient practice and a still continuing one.

Another old custom that has lingered on is the use of a go-between in arranging a marriage. Called a *nakōdo*, the matchmaker is generally the most illustrious man known to the family of the prospective groom. When he calls on the girl's family with a proposal of marriage, he is traditionally served a special kind of tea—a tea made of cherry blossoms. How do you make sakura tea? Well, when the trees are in bloom, you put the blossoms down in salt until they are (hopefully) needed. Then when you lay them carefully in a tea bowl and pour hot water over them, the blossoms unfold, and they are just as pink as the cheeks of the young lady while the nakōdo expatiates upon the merits of the man who would have her for his bride.

Although it is growing increasingly more frequent for a boy and a girl to take the matter into their own hands, the use of a go-between is still very common in Japan, and many parents still consider an arranged marriage the likeliest to be a successful one. As long as the nakōdo continues to exercise his good offices, so long will cherry blossoms continue to unfold their petals in the ceremonial tea bowls of Japan.

90. *The yamazakura* (*previous page*) of Mt. Yoshino is the most famous of cherry blossoms.

91-92. *Kimpusen-ji temple* stands at the top of Mt. Yoshino, to which mountain ascetics have been coming since the tenth century. Designated a National Treasure, the temple buildings were rebuilt in 1455, after having been destroyed by fire in 1348.

93-96. *Zaō-dō*, the main hall of Kimpusen-ji, is unique among temples in having the sakura design for its crest. Below left, water in the turtle-dragon's back, a symbol of longevity, is for rinsing the hands before praying. The hanging lantern (*right*) is called *sakuradōrō*, or cherry lantern. Banners (*below*) are donated to the temple by suppliants.

98-99. *Cherry blossoms, and the moon* rising over Mt. Yoshino (*overleaf*): the imperial court, the shogun and daimyos would make special trips to view them.

97. *Jizō* (*below*) is a bodhisattva who favors children, pregnant women, travelers and the wicked.